AR 3.7   pt. 0.5

GIANT TURTLE

LIVING THINGS

GIANT TURTLE

Rebecca Stefoff

BENCHMARK BOOKS

MARSHALL CAVENDISH
NEW YORK

Benchmark Books
Marshall Cavendish Corporation
99 White Plains Road
Tarrytown, New York 10591-9001

Illustrations by Jean Cassels

Library of Congress Cataloging-in-Publication Data
Stefoff, Rebecca, date
Giant turtle / by Rebecca Stefoff
p.   cm. — (Living things)
Includes bibliographical references (p.   ) and index.
Summary: Describes the physical characteristics, habitat, and behavior of a variety
of large turtles, including the green sea turtle, leatherback, and Galapagos tortoise.
ISBN 0-7614-0121-0 (lb)
1. Turtles—Juvenile literature. [1. Turtles.] I. Title.
II. Series: Stefoff, Rebecca, date Living things.
QL666.C5S765   1997   597.92—dc20   96-18483   CIP   AC

Photo research by Ellen Barrett Dudley

Cover photo: *Photo Researchers, Inc.*, M. Castro

The photographs in this book are used by permission and through the courtesy of:
Photo Researchers: Frans Lanting, 2, 8, 9, 10; Nigel J. Dennis, 11 (top);
Tom McHugh, 11 (bottom); Porterfield/Chickering, 16-17; Gilbert S. Grant, 20;
Jany Sauvanet, 21; S.E. Cornelius, 25 (top). *Animals Animals:* Breck P. Kent, 6;
Tui De Roy/Oxford Scientific Films, 12, 14 (top); Peter Weimann, 13; Jim Tuten,
14 (bottom); James D. Watt, 22; Konrad Wothe/Oxford Scientific Films, 24 (top);
Fred Whitehead, 24 (bottom); Adrienne T. Gibson, 32. *Tom Stack and Associates:*
Dave Fleetham, 7; Denise Tackett, 20. *Peter Arnold:* John Cancalosi, 13;
Roland Seitre, 15; Norbert Wu, 18, 23; Luiz C. Marigo, 19; Kelvin Aitken, 24-25;
Gerard Lacz, 25 (bottom); Lynda Richardson, 26 (left and right), 27.

Printed in the United States of America

3   5   6   4

For my mother

Galapagos tortoise

green sea turtle

Guess what? The turtle
munching that juicy green plant
is almost as tall as you are.

And the swimming turtle is so
big that you couldn't reach from
one end of its shell to the other.

These are the giant turtles of
land and sea.

Galapagos tortoise

Galapagos tortoise

Large, slow-moving turtles that live on land are called tortoises.

Tortoises are always at home, because they live in the hard shells that they carry around with them.

Tortoises have thick, stumpy legs like an elephant's. A tortoise needs strong legs to carry its heavy shell.

A tortoise can stretch its long, skinny neck w-a-a-y out to bite a tasty leaf . . .

. . . or pull its head inside its shell for safety.

Galapagos tortoises

Giant tortoises like hot weather. They live in tropical parts of the world. Some of them even live in deserts.

Sometimes giant tortoises get too hot. Then they crawl into muddy water holes to cool off.

Giant tortoises often gather in groups. If you saw a bunch of tortoises, would you think they were just big brown rocks?

10

African leopard tortoise

Aldabra tortoises

Galapagos tortoises

Most of the time tortoises get along well with each other. But once in a while they fight over food.

Fighting tortoises make themselves as tall as they can by stretching out their necks. They hiss and grunt, trying to scare each other. One tortoise will soon get tired of hissing and leave.

The winner will enjoy the tasty flower.

All tortoises are plant eaters. Some of them like to graze on the plants that grow in ponds.

Galapagos tortoises mating

When it is time for tortoises to have babies, a father and a mother come together for a few hours. Later the mother digs a hole and lays her eggs. Then she covers the eggs with leaves and dirt.

After six months or so, the baby tortoises peck their way out of the eggs. They look just like their parents—only much smaller. It will take twenty years for this tiny leopard tortoise to grow as large as its mother.

parent and baby leopard tortoises

Some of the largest turtles in the world live in the sea.

Sea turtles have shells, just like tortoises. But sea turtles can't pull their heads inside their shells, because their shells are flat. There's no room for the sea turtle's head inside.

The flat shell lets the sea turtle move swiftly through the water. Sea turtles can swim many miles in a day.

A sea turtle's legs are broad, flat flippers, with webs between the toes. These flippers don't work very well for walking on land, but they make the sea turtle a good swimmer.

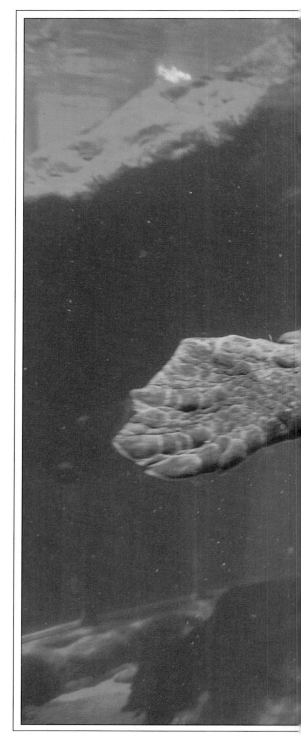

loggerhead sea turtle

green sea turtle

There are eight kinds of sea turtles in the world.

The green sea turtle is one of the largest sea turtles. It eats sea grass that grows in warm ocean waters around the world.

The green sea turtle is brown, not green. It got its name beause its meat looks green. People used to eat green sea turtles, but now many countries have laws against killing them.

The olive ridley is the smallest sea turtle—but it is still pretty big. A full-grown olive ridley weighs almost eighty pounds. Does it weigh more than you do?

olive ridley sea turtle

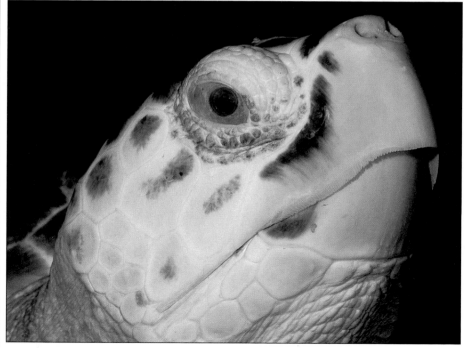

The hawksbill turtle has a sharp, curved beak like a hawk's bill.

It uses this beak to snip its favorite food, sponges, from the rocks.

The loggerhead turtle has strong jaw muscles. It uses its powerful jaws to crack open crabs and shells to get the meat inside.

The biggest turtle in the world is the leatherback. This leatherback has crawled up onto a sandy beach. Do you see the long ridges on its back? The leatherback is the only turtle with ridges like these on its shell.

leatherback sea turtle on beach

green sea turtle with cleaner fish

Little cleaner fish help sea turtles stay healthy. They eat the tiny animal pests that live on the turtle's skin. The cleaner fish know that the green sea turtle won't hurt them.

When the cleaner fish are finished with the green turtle, maybe they will work on this hawksbill turtle. It is too busy eating sponges to snap at them.

hawksbill turtle eating a sponge

Mother and father sea turtles mate in the water. Then the mother sea turtles crawl onto beaches to lay their eggs. This is the only time they leave the sea.

Sea turtles lay their eggs in the same place each year. Some beaches are crowded with hundreds of turtles digging their nests. A single nest can hold more than a hundred eggs.

mother sea turtle laying eggs

newly hatched loggerhead sea turtle

Baby turtles fresh from their eggs are called hatchlings. The hatchlings must hurry to the water before animals and birds snatch them up and eat them.

loggerhead hatchlings running to the sea

Even after a hatchling has reached the ocean, it is still not safe because of hungry fish. But slowly the little turtle will grow larger. By the time you are grown up, it will be one of the giants of the sea.

loggerhead hatchling's first swim

A QUICK LOOK AT THE GIANT TURTLE

All turtles belong to a large group of animals called reptiles. Snakes, lizards, crocodiles, and alligators are reptiles, too. Turtles are different from all other reptiles because their bodies are enclosed in shells. There are about 220 different kinds of turtles in the world. The largest ones are the eight kinds of sea turtles and some of the slow-moving land turtles known as tortoises.

Here are six giant turtles, with their scientific names in Latin and a few key facts.

GALAPAGOS TORTOISE

Chelonoidis elephantophus
(keh loh NOY dis eh leh FAN toh fus)
Found only on the Galapagos Islands, in the Pacific Ocean near South America. Males are larger than females and can weigh 400 to 500 pounds (180 to 225 kg). Known to live more than 100 years in zoos.

ANGONOKA TORTOISE

Asterochelys yniphon
(ahs teh ROH keh liss IN ih fon)
World's rarest and most endangered tortoise. Lives in a tiny part of Madagascar, an island near Africa. Fewer than 20 remain alive.

ALDABRA TORTOISE

Megalochelys gigantea
(meh gah LOH keh liss gye GAN tyah)
Native to Aldabra, in the Seychelles
Islands near East Africa. Now also
found on Zanzibar and Sri Lanka,
islands in the Indian Ocean. Largest
ever recorded weighed 560 pounds
(255 kg), with a 55-inch-long (1.4m)
shell.

LOGGERHEAD SEA TURTLE

Caretta caretta
(kah REH tah kah REH tah)
Grows to 450 pounds (200 kg) with a
shell 47 inches long (1.4 m). Nests
in Florida and South Africa. Lives
mostly in warm, shallow seas. Uses powerful
jaw muscles to crush crabs and other hard-
shelled sea animals.

GREEN SEA TURTLE

Chelonia mydas
(keh LOH nyah MYE das)
Second-largest sea turtle.
Average length of shell is 49 inches
(1.2 m). Nests in Central America,
Hawaii, Australia, and islands in
the Indian and Pacific oceans.
Swims rapidly. Has been known
to swim 300 miles (480 km)
in 10 days.

LEATHERBACK SEA TURTLE

Dermochelys coriacea

(der MOH keh liss cor YAY syuh)

World's largest turtle. Can weigh more than 1,000 pounds (450 kg), with shell 7 feet long (2.1 m). Prefers warm water but has been seen in oceans all around the world, except for polar regions. Nests in Central America and Southeast Asia.

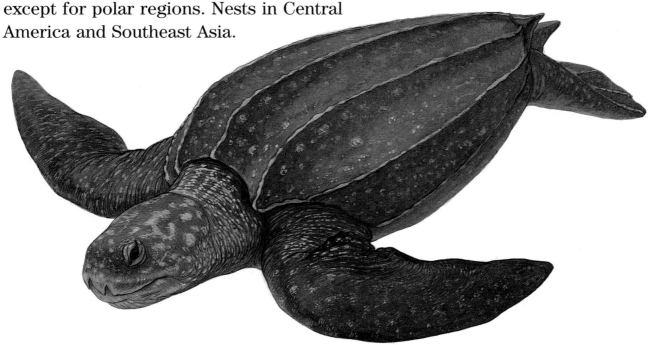

Taking Care of the Giant Turtle

Many giant turtles are in danger. People hurt sea turtles by catching them in fishing nets, by eating their eggs, by spilling oil and other poisons into the sea, and by building homes or hotels on the beaches where the turtles nest. People hurt land tortoises by destroying the places where they live, by making souvenirs from their shells, and by letting dogs and pigs eat the tortoises' eggs. Giant turtles need our protection now so that they will always be part a of life on land and in the sea.

Find Out More

Gibbons, Gail. *Sea Turtles.* New York: Holiday House, 1995.

Goode, John. *Turtles, Tortoises, and Terrapins.* New York: Scribner, 1971.

Papastavrou, Vassili. *Turtles and Tortoises.* New York: Bookwright Press, 1992.

Reeves, Martha Emilie. *The Total Turtle.* New York: Crowell, 1975.

Serventy, Vincent. *Turtle and Tortoise.* Milwaukee: Raintree Children's Books, 1992.

Index

Rebecca Stefoff has published many books for young readers. Science and environmental issues are among her favorite subjects. She lives in Oregon and enjoys observing the natural world while hiking, camping, and scuba diving.

Galapagos tortoise